IMAGES
of America
ALTOONA

On the Cover: This grocery was in the corner of the Lang Building at Second Street Southeast and First Avenue. It was purchased by John Swain in April 1911 from Sylvester Ferguson. The merchandise stocked included dry goods, shoes, groceries, chicken feed, and furnishings of all kinds. The clerks seen serving customers are Flo Reed and Errol Ferguson. The inventory was taken over by Leroy H. Battles in 1914. John Swain and his family moved in the summer of 1916 to California, where he opened another grocery store. (Courtesy of the Altoona Area Historical Society.)

IMAGES of America
ALTOONA

Alex Payne on behalf of the
Altoona Area Historical Society

Copyright © 2014 by Alex Payne on behalf of the Altoona Area Historical Society
ISBN 978-1-5316-6930-0

Published by Arcadia Publishing
Charleston, South Carolina

Library of Congress Control Number: 2013950198

For all general information, please contact Arcadia Publishing:
Telephone 843-853-2070
Fax 843-853-0044
E-mail sales@arcadiapublishing.com
For customer service and orders:
Toll-Free 1-888-313-2665

Visit us on the Internet at www.arcadiapublishing.com

To Karen Hanley and Dawn Bentley, who were great coauthors and researchers. I would have never been able to get this book done without you two.

Contents

Acknowledgments		6
Introduction		7
1.	Businesses	9
2.	Schools	39
3.	Churches and Organizations	53
4.	Events and Entertainment	65
5.	People and Homes	87
6.	Public Services	113
About the Altoona Area Historical Society		127

Acknowledgments

Since its incorporation as the official historical society of the city of Altoona in 2003, the Altoona Area Historical Society's collection has grown into a museum of stories, photographs, and artifacts depicting Altoona's history. We would like to thank all of the members of the Altoona Area Historical Society, members of the community, and the companies in the Altoona area for their help and support with this project.

We would like to specially thank former Altoona resident Mary Jane Johnson Buck for her help identifying people and places in our photographs along with helping us track down more images.

The research would have been almost impossible if it were not for Robert W. Thompson and his efforts to preserve Altoona's history.

We would also like to thank our special research assistant Jaiden Maestas, as well as our families and friends who have helped us as we have spent tireless hours and late nights working on this project.

We are grateful to those who opened their collections of photographs for us to use. A thanks goes to Tim Burget for all of the information and photographs he shared.

We would also like to thank Laura Duffield Biegger for sharing her family photographs with us. The staff at the Altoona Public Library has been amazing, as we worked sometimes from open to close.

The photographs used in this book are those of the Altoona Area Historical Society unless otherwise noted.

INTRODUCTION

Altoona's history starts out over 150 years ago. We usually start looking at the history of Altoona with Anthony Yant, who first settled in what is now Altoona in 1854. That same year, Gilbert T. Taylor settled there. The land was originally surveyed in 1847 and put up for sale by the US government in 1848, but it took six years to sell. After many different sales between different families, the Davis family ended up with the land on February 1, 1868.

The Davises hired surveyor Julian B. Bausman to lay out the city for them. He is also credited for giving the city its current name, Altoona. The city is named for the Latin word for "high," *altus*, after Bausman discovered that Altoona was the highest point on the Des Moines Valley Railroad between Des Moines and Keokuk.

The plot was recorded on July 30, 1868, and the post office opened the next day. When the Rock Island Railroad came to Altoona in September of that year, it referred to Altoona as Yant, the city's original name. Altoona was incorporated as a city on March 11, 1876.

As well as serving as Altoona's first mayor, Emory English was the town doctor, and after the great train crash of 1877, English was the first doctor on the scene.

Altoona's second mayor, Thomas Haines, is one of the best-known mayors of Altoona. Haines operated the T.E. Haines Tile and Brick Company. Haines is well known for the land he donated to the City of Altoona to be used as a city park, which is known as Haines Park.

The only other mayor of Altoona to have a park dedicated to him is Leslie J. "Sam" Wise. Wise brought advanced thinking to his position as mayor by paving the streets of Altoona, building a sewer system that was advanced for its time, and allowing for future expansion. His dedication to Altoona's parks lead to the city's sports complex being named Sam Wise Youth Complex.

By 1900, Altoona could almost be classified as a coal camp. United Mine Workers of America Local 407 was organized in Altoona in 1897, and by 1902, it had 61 members. This is close to 20 percent of the population at the time.

The T-51, the first color printer that could print more than one color in a single pass, was invented in Altoona. The first acre of hybrid seed corn was grown in Altoona. The revolutionary portable pitching mound and Flex-A-Clay baseball sand were also invented in Altoona.

With Iowa's first municipal airport, Altoona became a place Iowans looked to for entertainment. Adventureland Amusement Park, Adventure Bay Water Park, the former Otter Mountain Amusement/Water Park, and Prairie Meadows Race Track and Casino have kept Altoona at the forefront for entertainment in Iowa. With Facebook's new data centers built in Altoona, the Shoppes at Prairie Crossing, and Bass Pro Shops, Altoona is set to offer Iowans more than ever before. It is all a reflection of the history of this amazing community.

On May 5, 2003, the Altoona City Council recognized the Altoona Area Historical Society as the city's official organization to collect, secure, and preserve the artifacts and records of the city of Altoona and surrounding areas.

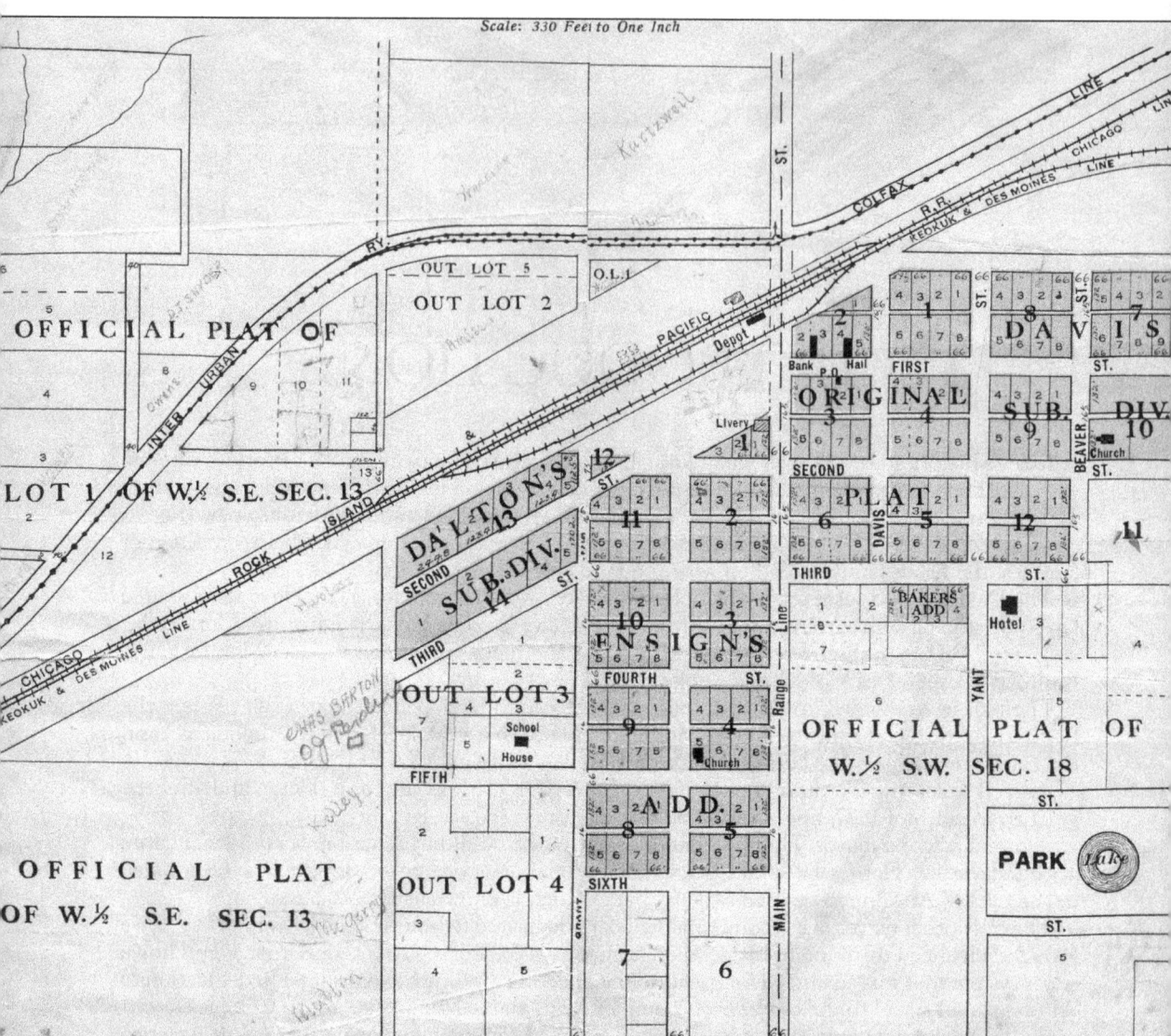

This plat map of Altoona shows many interesting places. Notice the businesses included in this map: the livery in the center and the bank in the upper right, as well as a hall, two churches, the school, and the Haines Hotel. Also pictured in the lower right is the man-made lake at Haines Park. The lake was dredged from a shallow slough and was deep enough for swimming and boating. There were three railroad lines serving Altoona: Colfax Interurban; Chicago, Rock Island & Pacific Railroad; and the Keokuk and Des Moines Railway line. In the upper middle of the map, the George Kurtzweil 40-acre property is noted. This field included a one-acre plot where George Kurtzweil produced the nation's first commercial hybrid seed corn. Kurtzweil went on to become one of the founders of Pioneer Hi-Bred Corn Company, now called DuPont Pioneer.

One

BUSINESSES

The grain elevator in this sketch was owned by T.E. Haines. He came to Altoona in 1868 as a grain dealer, and soon after, he built the steam-powered, 10,000-bushel grain elevator that sat directly across from the Rock Island Depot. Although the elevator was torn down in 1940, the grain bins remain and are part of the present-day Farmers Cooperative.
The drawing was featured in the 1875 *Andreas Atlas*.

After the Macklin House burned in 1899, Altoona was left with no hotel. Thomas Haines stepped up to the plate and started construction in 1902 on new accommodations he named the Haines Park Hotel, located at 403 Third Avenue. The hotel contained 20 guest rooms. Steam heat was installed at the cost of $500. Expense was not spared, and details such as a gold leaf sign adorned the hotel. Overnight guests, as well as boarders, were welcome to stay. Opening day was April 24, 1903, and contained much fanfare. The ladies of the Altoona Christian Church served an "excellent chicken dinner" for 35¢. Gov. Albert Cummings came to the hotel with the ministerial club for a banquet, as did other famous Iowans, such as the Younker brothers. Sold after Haines's death, the hotel was moved to its present location in 1912 and sits on the corner of Second Street and Second Avenue. It has since been home to the Elizabeth Nursing Home, the Amish Pantry Restaurant, and apartments.

This is Second Street Southeast, known at the time of the picture as Main Street. The tallest building is Porter Hardware. A December 1924 implement journal told of Jesse Porter having a great year selling farm machinery. There are seven McCormick-Deering tractors shown here ready for pickup. According to the article, Porter previously had six tractors delivered. He also had nine corn picker orders during this time.

As part of his advertising for the farm machinery he sold, Jesse Porter of Porter Hardware had pictures taken out in the field. In 1917, he advertised Hayes corn planters, 120-tooth steel harrows, three types of cultivators, and Sattley and P.O. gang plows. He sold McCormick-Deering Farmall tractors in 1935.

The Lang Building was constructed in 1904 by Dr. Corvus Lang. Dr. Lang married Grace Swain in 1894. He was a physician and surgeon in Altoona before his marriage. With partner Aquilla Duesning, Dr. Lang erected the building on the lot where the Macklin House, a hotel, had burned in 1899. It was at the southeast corner of Second Street and First Avenue. While brick sidewalks were advocated by the city council, Lang and Duesning were able to have the city council add an amendment to the ordinance to also include the cement sidewalk they wanted to put around their building. They had a board awning along the west side of the structure. By 1927, the building had been condemned as unsafe.

Porter Hardware was located in the eastern portion of the first floor of the Lang Building, replaced by the Class Act Productions (CAP) Community Theatre building. The Lang Building was a two-story brick structure housing a grocery store along with Porter Hardware. In the above photograph, note the barrel churn in the foreground. It is one of the many different items offered for sale at the time by Porter. The business was started in 1902 by Jesse Porter in a partnership with his brother C.D. Porter. The business was first located at 106 Second Street Southeast in Altoona. Note the wide arrange of products offered at the time. Brands such as Moon Brothers Buggies, Riverside Stoves, Standard Sewing Machines, Coles Hot Blast Stoves, and Stevens Rifles are advertised in these photographs. Porter Hardware would move into the R.A. Crawford Building, east of the Lang Building, the current home of the Altoona Area Historical Museum.

Jason C. Mason, editor-publisher from 1900 to 1945, and an unidentified woman stand in front of the old *Altoona Herald* office in the early 1900s. This building stood on Second Street Southeast in the current Olde Town section of Altoona. While Mason headed the paper, every day at 10:00 a.m. he would say, "Time to eat," and everyone from the *Altoona Herald* enjoyed coffee and cookies.

James C. Mason stands in the back room of the *Altoona Herald* office about 1910. The view faces toward the front of the building. The ornate tin ceiling remains in the building, which is now occupied by the Insurance Station, Inc. The *Altoona Herald* was established as the *Altoona Rustler* in 1889 by B.W. Henry and was sold to Emory and Arthur English in November of that same year.

Farm sales were advertised in the newspaper to entice neighbors and area people. Ladies of one of the churches close by would fix lunch, and there would be a cashier or clerk for collecting the money in addition to an auctioneer. Neighbors met for a day of socializing as well as purchasing.

Farm sales were the way farmers sold their livestock, machinery, and other items when they gave up farming and moved to town. At this sale, hardware store owner Jesse Porter uses his truck to advertise his business to all his neighbors and others who were at the sale.

This is picture of bank owner Lewis "L.O." Shaffer, his son Norman, and cashier Carl Altman in front of the Shaffer State Bank, located on the north side of business district. This picture was taken in June 1927. The bank was known as the Citizens Bank and was purchased by Shaffer in 1900. He installed a new bank counter and enclosed the banking department with a teller cage. In 1914, it was incorporated and the name was changed to Shaffer State Bank. Robert "R.A." Crawford served as vice president. The Shaffer State Bank fell victim to the Great Depression, as did many other businesses. In 1934, the bank's board of directors asked the state superintendent of banking to take over management for the purpose of liquidation. The notice was published in the paper and effective as of May 24, 1934. The little town of Altoona was left without a bank.

CITIZENS-BANK
ALTOONA-IOWA

Pictured here is the interior of Citizens Bank. After purchasing the bank, Lewis "L.O." Shaffer opened for business on Monday, July 2, 1900, in one corner of his drugstore where the banking business was conducted for several years. He bought the Altoona Exchange Bank from R.A. Crawford in 1901, which included the safe and bank fixtures, the business, and the goodwill of the concern. Shaffer finally found his banking business growing and demanding his entire attention, so in 1908, he disposed of his drugstore and erected the building on the corner of First Avenue and Second Street. Shaffer made a promotional offer to every boy who opened a savings account on March 16, 1912, by including the incentive of an Ingersoll Yankee watch. The second floor of the Citizens Bank was remodeled to a suite of five rooms in January 1918.

G&G Grocery, located at 301 First Avenue South, was originally the Altoona Grocery and was run by Harry Hollingsworth. In April 1931, it was bought by Charles Graves and Harry Gibson, and the name was then changed to the G&G Grocery. The store's phone number was 35, and it offered delivery. Pearl Hazen and Mildred Tiller were clerks over the years. During the Depression, Charley Graves built a structure beside the store where he kept scarce items. When a preferred customer asked for one of those items, he would leave his store through the back door, go next door, and get the item without anyone realizing he had visited his safe storage place. The building was owned by Clark Pearson and, later, his grandson Melvin Proudfit. This picture was taken on March 19, 1939. The structure was on a prime corner in Altoona and was torn down for a newer business building. (Courtesy of Karen Hanley.)

This is the intersection of First Avenue South, running horizontally, and Third Street Southwest and Southeast, which were dirt roads in 1939. On the left, the little building is the icehouse. Directly behind it is a service garage with one gas pump, and next to it is a blacksmith shop. In the center with the awning is the G&G Grocery. The building to the right is the home of Anna Ingle. (Courtesy of Karen Hanley.)

W. H. BOOTH, M. D.,
Physician & Surgeon,
ALTOONA, IOWA.

CALLS PROMPTLY ATTENDED, DAY AND NIGHT.

William H. Booth was born in 1852 in Iowa, probably in Jasper County, where he was living with his parents in 1856. In 1876, he married Elizabeth White. He went to the University of Iowa Medical College, from which he graduated in 1877. That same year, he established his medical practice in Altoona on Main Street. Around 1900, he moved his family to Oregon, where he died in 1914.

This 1917 view of the Altoona depot on the Rock Island Railroad looks south. This building was located directly north of the old Burget Mill building on First Avenue South. A portion of the Altoona Manufacturing Co. building and O.H. Pearson's Elevator can be seen in the background.

This c. 1968 view of the Rock Island Depot shows that both the baggage room and wooden platform have been removed. The depot was built on the west side of First Avenue. The bay window situated on the track side is where the telegrapher/dispatcher/agent sat to see the trains coming from either direction. Two of the men that held the position include Byron Delaney and Noah Lacey.

This car is at the Altoona depot on the Des Moines & Central Iowa Interurban on its way from Des Moines to Colfax. There were six intermediate stops. On September 11, 1902, passenger service began on the leg finished between Des Moines and Altoona at 20¢ each way. The trains ran every hour and 40 minutes, increasing shortly to every half hour on weekends. In 1939, new cars were put into service. The new cars were much longer than the old ones and were built of all steel, capable of making much better speed. They also featured much better seating facilities. They were much stronger and easier riding than the previous ones. The cars were divided into three compartments—one for baggage, a smoker compartment, and the passenger compartment—with a heating plant of either hot water or electricity and a modern toilet room to the rear of the car. The Rock Island Railroad tracks were just south of the interurban, and it was possible for freight cars to transfer between lines.

Martin Johnson, a track supervisor for the Rock Island Railroad, stands with his motorcar in 1939. The motorcar was kept in a shed about a block or two east of the depot. As a track supervisor, Johnson had a run he would take three times a week. He was on the "KD run" between Keokuk and Des Moines and inspected the tracks and signals. He would leave Monday morning and go to Keokuk, where he would stay the night in a train motel and come back Tuesday. Johnson repeated this trek Wednesday to Thursday and Friday to Saturday. He started working for the Rock Island Railroad with a pick and shovel at the age of 17. Johnson and his family lived in Altoona between 1937 and 1947 before moving to Des Moines, Kansas, California, and eventually back to their hometown of Iowa Falls. (Courtesy of Mary Jane Johnson Buck.)

This early view of Second Street looking east includes the J.N. Swain Grocery and Porter Hardware, which occupy the Lang Building on the far right. Notice how the town comes to an abrupt stop just a few buildings down. There is very interesting advertising on the buildings and in the windows promoting acetylene lights, cream separators, Mitchell- and Weber-brand wagons, buggies, gasoline engines, dry goods, groceries, shoes, and Gold Medal flour. The Swain store advertised green stamps, which were given for purchases made and redeemable for merchandise out of a catalog. Also, note the Success Camp (Modern Woodmen of America) sign in the upstairs window of the Lang Building. Local social organizations occupied the upstairs of the structure and the R.A. Crawford Building. The R.A. Crawford Building is now home to the Altoona Area Historical Museum. This picture was taken before 1912.

In 1890, the Shaffer Drug Store carried books, musical instruments, school supplies, jewelry, and furniture in addition to drugs. In 1900, Shaffer started the Citizens Bank in part of the drugstore. After he bought the Altoona Exchange Bank, he put the fixtures in the drugstore. He disposed of the drugstore in 1908, finding his banking business took all of his time. It was purchased by Claud and James Casebeer.

Standing in front of the Porter Garage are, from left to right, owner Arthur "Toad" Porter, longtime employee Austin Walters, an unidentified man, Henry Gifford, and Herbert Ewing. The photograph was taken in 1923. The garage was a good place for residents to meet and catch up on local happenings.

Above is the service garage of Toad Porter. He built the original garage in 1920 and the one seen above in 1926. Toad's son Neill joined him in the business. When his father retired, Neill took over the business and continued it into the 1980s as Porter's Auto Parts, offering supplies and automobile services. Neill's brother-in-law Lee Anderson joined him as his partner. Products sold by the garage included Wickey, "the modern battery, they cannot be frozen;" Iowa Tires, "they wear out, they don't blow out;" and Texaco motor oil, "crank-proof." An extra service was also provided—old tires brought 5¢ at Porter's garage in 1932. The garage had a catchy pitch for service: "Give a girl a ring, thrills her to pieces, but Mister! You should see the big kick your car would get out of a whole new set of rings."

This was the blacksmith shop of Nicholas Hemstreet, who began practicing his trade in Sylvester, Wisconsin. In 1868, he brought his family to Altoona, where he operated a dry goods store. His blacksmith barn in Altoona was west of the Christian church.

Roy Davis Sr.'s service station, the White Way Sinclair Station, was situated at the corner of First Avenue and Eighth Street and is seen here about 1932. Davis Sr. opened this station in 1927 and later owned other area service stations. The car belongs to longtime Altoona resident Bill Newell. The teddy bear was Newell's trademark. A hold-up one night in 1940 netted the robbers $25 in cash and a few checks from this station.

Warren Hatchery, started by Clarence Warren, was passed to son Edwin in 1948. Edwin took the business from egg incubators to custom grinding and feed mixing to making noodles in 1960. Ed and his sister Vi developed the recipe that was marketed under the name Aunt Vi's Noodles. In 2003, Warren Frozen Foods, which produced frozen egg noodles and pasta, became part of Marzetti Food Service. (Courtesy of Warren family.)

This building, which was under construction in 1947 and 1948, still stands today at 709 Second Avenue Southwest. It actually faces Eighth Street, which is the old Highway 6. The occupant was United Sales and Service, who sold old and new appliances including the One Minute Washer, American Standard bathroom fixtures, and RCA TVs. Plumbing and heating services were offered as well.

The storefront of Knights Variety Fabric & Clothing Shop, shown in this picture, is decorated for the Altoona centennial. The store was in operation from 1969 to 1973. Knight's Variety Fabric & Clothing Shop was located at 305 First Avenue South. It was owned by Arlene Knight. The store carried fabric and notions as well as clothing and even penny candy. The store offered Regal stamps with each purchase.

Kent Gage opened the Kent Feed in Indianola in 1927. He began manufacturing a healthy feed called Baby Beef, which contained no fillers. Most feed had low nutritional value. The Altoona plant employees have always stood behind farmers. During a month-long program in 1971, Altoona Kent Feed employees pledged to eat pork five times a week to help increase pork prices, which were at a five-year low.

The Masonic lodge was built in 1888 by D.W. Ainey using brick from the T.E. Haines Tile and Brick Company. The Masons constructed the second story for their lodge at a cost of $1,335 and conducted meetings there. The lodge's regular meeting night was Wednesday on or preceding the full moon. This necessitated members to consult an almanac instead of a calendar, and occasionally, there were two meetings in one month. In 1921, the regular meeting date was set as the second Wednesday of the month. In 1950, the building was remodeled, and the Masons occupied both stories. The front was remodeled in 1962. They vacated the building in 1968 and moved to a new location on the east side of Altoona. Today, Borseth Properties, Ltd., owns the building, which is now home to the Borseth Law Office.

The town of Altoona was talking about building a canning factory as early as 1903. The pluses were addition to the tax base, employment, and income for the surrounding area farmers. The factory was built in 1917. By August of that year, the machinery was being installed in the building. There were 1,400 acres of corn contracted for with area farmers in 1919. The usual run of the factory started the last week of August (during the week of the local fair) and lasted six

weeks. The plant ran into the 1940s. Approximately 30,000 gallons of water were used each day. A shortage of water plagued the factory during its entire lifetime and was the main reason the factory never expanded. Besides several wells being dug, water was imported from Des Moines via tank cars on the interurban. The whole canning process took three hours.

Ray Burget stands outside of the Burget Mill building at 106 First Avenue South in 1959. The business adapted to the changing times, hauling coal during the Depression and selling hay to the Army during World War II. The building was sold in 2001, and grandson Tim Burget bought it back in 2012. The original wood siding remains on the building, and oats can still be found inside many of the walls. (Courtesy of Tim Burget.)

Workmen at the Burget Mill building help with the addition made to the building after it was moved from the corner of First Street Southeast and Fourth Avenue to its current location at 106 First Avenue South. The area to the right (the front of the structure) was added on after the building was pulled down the street by tractors and oxen in the 1930s. (Courtesy of Tim Burget.)

Denniston & Partridge Co., a lumber company, started in 1902 by purchasing the W.H. West lumberyard. Within two years, they opened up a larger business in the lumber trade. They stocked lumber, building materials, fence posts, pulleys, shingles, lime, brick plaster, and cement. The company was sold in the late 1900s to the Gilchrist/Jewett Lumber Company.

Burget Mill has been in business in Altoona since 1896. It is the oldest family-owned business in Altoona and is still in operation today. It opened the Country Store at 200 First Avenue South on March 30, 1985. It still used the 106 First Avenue South location until that was sold in 2001. The company slowly moved all operations to the 200 First Avenue South location. This picture was taken in 1968.

This 1968 photograph shows the Haines Park Hotel and *Altoona Herald* office. The wraparound porch of the hotel has been removed, and today, the building houses apartments. The *Altoona Herald* office was moved from Second Street to Eighth Street and then to the downtown *Des Moines Register* location in 2012.

This view of Second Street Southeast shows many businesses that existed in 1968. Jeffords Meat Locker, owned by Clem Jefford, is shown to the left in the picture along with a barbershop and the Masonic lodge. The right side of the picture features the Porter Hardware building and the American Legion hall to the right of the hardware store.

This is the former Hy-Vee grocery store at 629 Eighth Street Southeast, situated on the north side of the road. It was built in 1960, and today, it is the Pat Barton Dance Studio. Hy-Vee is now at the southwest corner of First Avenue South and Eighth Street Southwest. (Courtesy of Hy-Vee.)

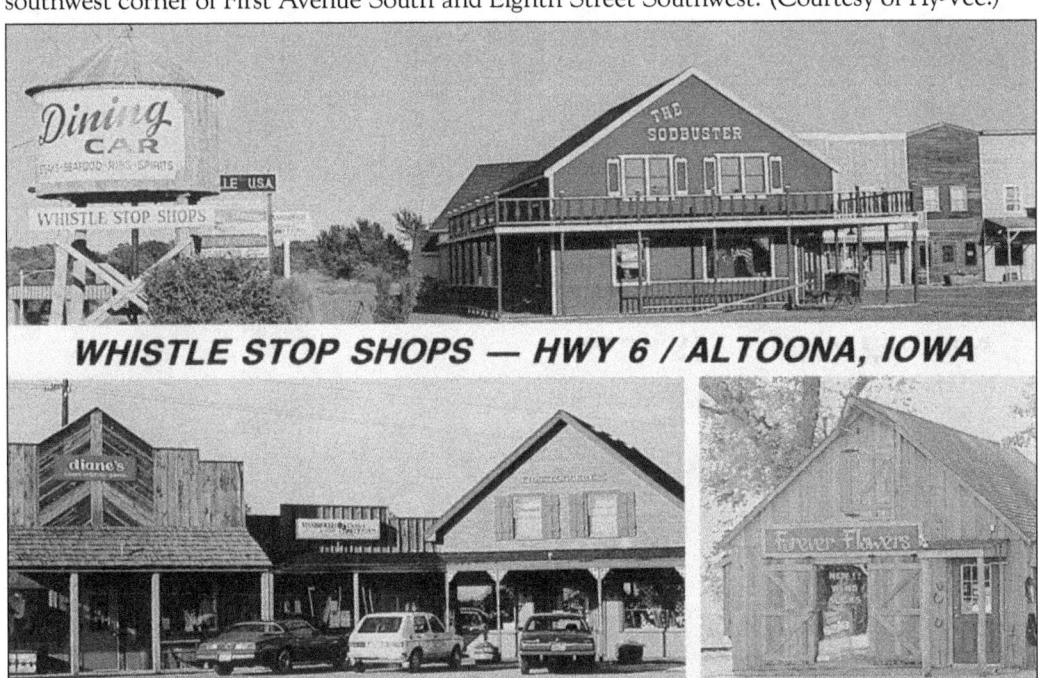

The Whistle Stop Shops opened in the 1970s and featured clothing stores Diane's, Kids Toggery, and the Sodbuster. Stanbrough Realtors and Forever Flowers were also located in the shopping center. The Dining Car was a popular restaurant that featured a 1912 railroad dining car. The space was needed when Anthony's Lounge planned a 17,000-square-foot addition for a dance floor and bandstand. (Courtesy of Alex Payne.)

Bob Townsend, the man behind Townsend Industries, was a small printing shop owner who addressed a need for a color press attachment for offset print presses. He developed this invention to assist his work in the direct mail business. He had machine shop training plus degrees in engineering and business. Pictured on the right is the T-51 color press attachment in 1957. It enabled the use of two colors in one pass. Manufacturing of the T-51 began in 1959. Instead of expanding to other products and diversifying, the company grew and survived with its single product. It made various models to fit the variety of presses. With today's technology, this invention is not in as much demand. In the picture at left is Danny Guy (left) with Kelley Adey, and below is Bob Gaudette, all Townsend employees.

Shown in this photograph are representatives of the Townsend Industries at a trade show. The company, established in 1957 by Robert T. Townsend, was built from the ground up and manufactured printing trade machinery parts and attachments. The company also provided contract manufacturing services in the Midwest, specializing in CNC turning machines and powder coating. The expertise developed over 40 years made it one of the top manufacturers of offset printing equipment in the world. By 1987, the company grew to 1,300 distribution and service outlets and exports to 47 countries. There were 18 employees in the Altoona plant. The company was always privately owned, and employees were shown appreciation for their hard work. Every year, they were taken on a fishing trip to Canada with all expenses paid. Robert Townsend passed away in 2010. The company ended operations on June 17, 2010, after over 50 years in business.

Bob and Ruth Moffitt purchased the Mitchellville Funeral Home in 1947. Bob and Ruth Moffitt opened a second funeral home in Altoona in 1965 in this former private residence at 105 Fourth Street Southwest. Hamilton's Funeral Home of Des Moines purchased both Moffitt Funeral Homes in 1976 and continues to provide families with service needs, including cremation. A total remodel of this funeral home was finished in 2012. (Courtesy of Hamilton's Funeral Home.)

This is a 1940s view of the northeast side of Second Street Southeast. The far right building is the Yount's grocery store, built in 1922, now Olde Town Tap. To the left of Yount's is the city hall building, which housed the fire department until 1962. When the fire department moved to its new building, the former area was remodeled to serve as the council chambers.

Two

Schools

In the "Bee Hive" school during the 1880s, the second floor of the building was finished so that there was one large room and two recitation rooms. A third teacher was hired, and then, the school was divided into three departments: primary, intermediate, and high school. The principal taught high school at a salary of $55 per month in 1896, with the other classes being taught by women receiving $30 per month.

There is no public record indicating how the school system in Altoona was established. This building is referred to as the Bee Hive school. It was erected in 1878 and used until 1909. Prior to this structure, classes had been taught in a storeroom on the second floor of the G.W. Strong Building on Second Street Southeast.

Seen here on a stage strewn with flowers is Altoona High School's graduating class in 1901. The ceremony was at the Christian church. Pictured from left to right are Ivy Perdue, Norman Shaffer, Birdella Love, principal George Ogden, and Genesta London. The class motto, sewn overhead on the curtain, is "Launched But Not Anchored."

This school portrait of the Altoona School, featuring grades fifth through eighth, was taken in 1927. From left to right are (first row) two unidentified students, Melvin Wheeler, Vivian Brundage, Doris Mae Kurtzweil, Elia Lee, Margerite Parker, Dorothy Scoley, Okel Porter, Anne Heller, Elizabeth Lee, Margaret Strain, and Alta Black; (second row) Harold Barbon, unidentified, Lewis Heller, Melvin Olson, Raymond Renaud, Gladine Hartline, Genevieve McKowan, Mary Oglevie, Hazel Warren, Christine Hartline, and Violet Eastep; (third row) Robert Thompson, Donald Minick, Alice Kelly, Wanda Ewing, three unidentified students, Edith Huffman, Alice Minick, unidentified, Alma Olson, Claude Snyder, Neil Porter, George McKowan, and Chick Heller Jr. This picture was taken in the fall, as evidenced by the clothes. It also shows a vast variety of clothing styles and represents the range of income levels that existed within Altoona during this time. Note the young lady in the wheelchair who had polio on the right side of the picture. It proves how progressive Altoona was with including students with disabilities in the classroom.

This building was constructed in 1909 at a cost of $9,000. Bricklayer and dormer expert Berge Pace constructed the building. It became a fully accredited school offering four years of high school in 1919. The high school had 19 students in 1916 and over 50 in 1918.

In 1924, the school board proposed a $36,000 bond issue to remodel and add more classrooms as well as a gymnasium. The *Altoona Herald* suggested that if each man smoked one less cigar a week, he would have enough for his share of the taxes due to the bond. The bond did not pass at this time. This photograph was taken around 1927.

Norma Champion Stuart played on the Altoona High School basketball team from 1944 to 1948. She was a forward whose highest-scoring game was 22 points. Women's basketball was six on six, meaning there were three forwards and three guards. Only forwards were allowed to shoot the ball, and guards played defense. (Courtesy of Mary Jane Johnson Buck.)

In 1939, the current gymnasium/auditorium was built with assistance from the federal Works Progress Administration. The jobs program was instituted during the Depression to provide work for unemployed Americans. The gymnasium is the only original part of the Altoona school to remain. The school is currently used as an elementary school only.

ALTOONA HIGH SCHOOL

FOOTBALL

ADULT SEASON TICKET

Name _____

Good For All Three Home Games

60c   1   2   3   1932

As shown on the football ticket above, the cost of three home games was 60¢. In 1932, high school football was a serious thing. The players were on a strict training schedule set up by their coach. No school parties were held during the football season. A school party was deemed as such if it was approved by faculty and chaperoned by a class sponsor. Parents were asked to limit their kids' social activities, and players were expected to be off the streets by 9:00 p.m. Two nights before a game, players were expected to be in bed by 9:00 p.m.

The 1946 Altoona football team pictured includes, from left to right, (first row) Don Stivers, Bob Barton, Gene Harding, and Jerry Mills; (second row) Rudy Halterman, Gerold Olson, Ed Poweshiek, Marvin McCrackin, and Conley Slutts; (third row) Don Callison, John LeCroy, Chuck Davis, Dutch Van Dusseldorp, and school superintendent, math teacher, and football coach James J. Mills.

The Fourth of July baseball games were always a big attraction in Altoona. They included a mixed bag of players from high school to middle age. This 1920s picture shows how different the gloves were for the players, and only wooden bats were available. The 1920s were considered the golden age of baseball due to the interest Babe Ruth drew to the sport.

This picture of the Altoona High School students was taken while Paul Sonner was superintendent, sometime between 1925 and 1928. Notice the high-laced boots of the gentlemen in the first row. It was popular for both males and females to wear ties at this time. The young man in the forth row has a large "A" on his own sweater. The teachers pictured are John Houlette, Helen Stookey, and F. Vandermast.

The Altoona High School girls' glee club of the 1934–1935 school year is pictured here. They are, from left to right, (first row) Marion Harris, Jean Warren, Barbara Heller, and Vera Garrett; (second row) Helen Johnson, Marjorie Hick, Grace Hart, June Thayer, June Thompson, and Dorothy DeMoss; (third row) Velda Thornton, Francis Vance, Grace Warren, Darlene Plummer, Marjorie Owens, and Nina West. In November 1934, this group presented the two-act play *The Feast of The Red Corn*, directed by teacher Helen Johnson.

This late-1930s Altoona school picture is a classic example of life during that time. Note that most of the boys wear bib overalls, while some don the basic blues and others sport their Sunday best striped overalls. Some are dressed in sweater vests or shirts, and some even have ties. Many of the girls have dresses make from feed sacks, usually designed in a floral pattern.

The girls' kitten ball (also known as softball) team of the 1934–1935 season is seen here. From left to right are Nina West, Grace Warren, Marion Harris, June Thayer, June Thompson, Vera Garret, Wilma Silver, Velda Thornton, Margaret Mason, Francis Vance, Barbara Heller, and Darlene Plummer. These girls' ages range from 13 to 17 years old. The boys had kitten ball teams as well.

This is the Altoona High School graduating class of 1948. From left to right are (first row) Al Olson, Gene Harding, Jeanette Walton, Marilyn Cresap, and Joe Norton; (second row) Leota Mott, Norma Champion, valedictorian Carolyn LeCroy, Marilyn Shultice, Lois Michael, Natalie Scharf, and Mary Jane Johnson; (third row) Robert Barton, Robert Kraemer, and Jack Warren. Norma Brown was not able to attend due to having the mumps. The class motto was "Take the steps to success, the elevator is not working." The Altoona High School colors were purple and gold at this time. They were changed to black and gold when the school system merged all of the schools in the southeast part of Polk County. The senior class play was *Love Is Too Much Trouble*, and the commencement address was "What are you standing for?" by Earl S. Kelp of Drake University. Commencement was held on May 21, 1948, at 8:00 p.m. in the school auditorium. (Courtesy of Mary Jane Johnson Buck.)

There were three Nebo schools. The first school burned, and the second school was on land that was sold, but the new owners did not want the school land taken out of their parcel. A third Nebo school was located south of Twenty-seventh Street about a quarter mile west of the road on Northeast Sixty-forth Street. The school had separate doors and cloak rooms for boys and girls on the east side of the building. There was one large classroom. A well on the property provided water that was carried to the school building and poured into a large crock. A button at the bottom of the crock dispensed water, and each child had his or her own cup. A hot meal was supplied by the parents once a week during the winter. Heat for the school was provided by a large wood stove (and a coal stove in later years). This picture was taken in the early 1920s.

Carnival!

By The Altoona School

Thursday Evening, December 19

IN THE SCHOOL BUILDING

Benefit of Athletic Association

LOTS OF FUN and EATS

Admission : : : : 10c and 15c

Includes Admission to vaudiville show

School carnivals to benefit the athletic association were a common occurrence in the 1930s, and Altoona school carnivals were no exception. One popular attraction noted in the newspaper was a ring toss about the necks of live ducks swimming in a large tank. Other attractions were bands, boxing matches, fortune-telling booths, and movie screenings for the children. Local businesses supplied prizes that were given away throughout the evening.

Mary Jane Johnson models her band uniform, made by Nellie Porter. It was made of white satin with gold stars. Band concerts were held on Second Street Southeast once a week in the summer. A hayrack was pulled onto the street and used as a stage. The soda fountain at Wilbern Drug sold snacks during the concerts. After each piece of music was presented, the cars' horns were honked in approval. (Courtesy of Mary Jane Johnson Buck.)

This is a sketch of Largey School, built one mile west of Altoona. It was modeled after a schoolhouse in Pisa, Italy, and plans were drawn by Norman T. Vorse. There were three rooms on the upper floor: a classroom, a library, and a room used as a kitchen with cupboards for dishes. School children often had hot lunches when mothers brought food at noon. On the lower floor were sinks for washing up, the furnace room, and the coal room. Warm water for washing hands was heated by the teacher or students, and the toilets were outside. Zona Mae Smith was the school's teacher from 1916 to 1929. During the 1940s, Ora Johnson, Virginia Jeffries, and Hilda Boys were teachers. Dorothy Poortinga taught during the 1949–1950 school term. The school is seen here at Seventh Avenue Southwest and Eighth Street Southwest. The school is no longer standing today.

Shown here are the 1968 Southeast Polk graduates living in second district of Southeast Polk, consisting of Altoona and Clay Township. Pictured are principal Don Kiester and Supt. Charles Varner. There were 176 graduates in the class of 1968. Southeast Polk was formed July 1, 1962. The formation of Southeast Polk took many years and is considered one of the longest school merger fights in Iowa history. Three elections, a myriad of law suits, and two Iowa Supreme Court opinions were involved in the lengthy process. The majority of the opposition came from the citizens of Pleasant Hill. In the election, only one citizen in Pleasant Hill voted for the formation of the new district. Eleven school districts were merged into the new district. Finding a location for the high school was another issue. The citizens of Altoona wanted the junior-senior high school to be built close to Altoona, but the final decision was to erect the school at the geographical center of the district. A $1.9-million junior-senior high school opened during the 1964–1965 school year.

Three

Churches and Organizations

A wooden building for the Christian church was constructed in Altoona in 1872. Also that year, a Cincinnati foundry cast a brass church bell that rang out loud and clear until 1911, when the new brick church was constructed. That original church building was remodeled into a house that still stands at 401 Third Street Southeast.

Before the Methodist and Christian churches, the two denominations were organized in Altoona, and religious meetings were held for all those of faith jointly at the Woodrow School House, which was one mile north of the Altoona Cemetery. In July 1867, twenty-six interested people indicated their willingness to form a congregation. A wooden building for the Christian church was constructed in 1872. This picture of the Christian church congregation was taken between

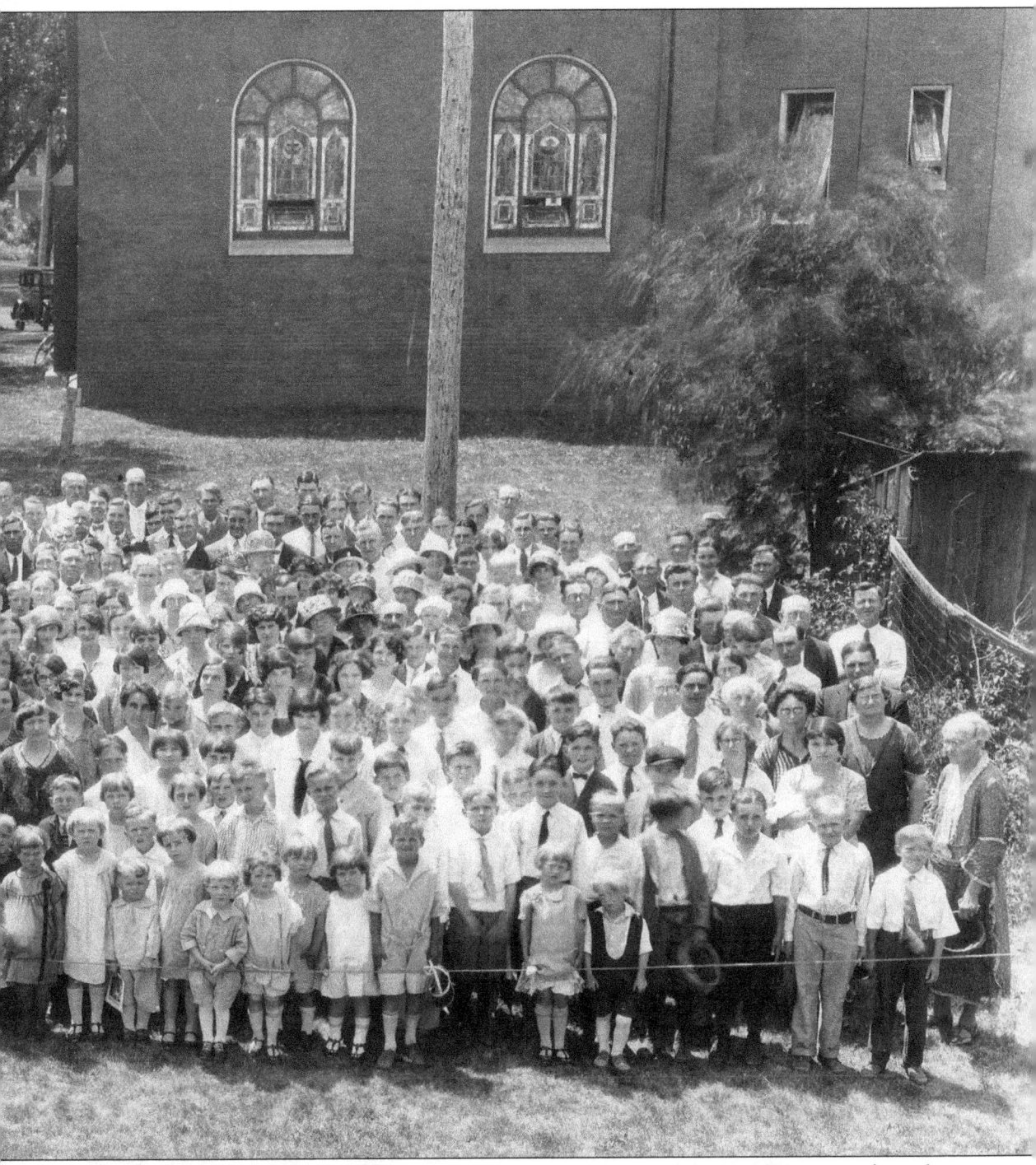

1926 and 1929, at the time R.R. Marken was minister. A series of three pictures was taken of the congregation: one of the men, one of the women and children, and the one above. This was the second building for the Christian church, and it was located on the corner of Third Street Southeast and Second Avenue Southeast.

Altoona Christian Church was also known as the Church of Christ. The church building was finished in 1872, and it was enlarged in 1880. That church had special problems with the pews being so close to the front door that it was hard to bring a casket inside. In 1910, the congregation started planning a new church building. The organizers behind the church building included banker Norman B. Shaffer, William Iseminger, the Reverend L.G. Parker, Albert Yount, *Altoona Herald* publisher James C. Mason, and Albert N. Immel. The 1910 church was at the northwest corner of Third Street Southeast and Second Avenue Southeast at 105 Third Street Southeast. It was dedicated on April 2, 1911.

The members of the sixth-grade Sunday school class at the Methodist Episcopal church seen here around 1959 are, from left to right, Carla Henry, Janice Milbourne, Cindy Harrell, Judy Calbreath, Betty Ballard, Bill Guesford, Robert Raitt, Bobby McGreen, Dennis Calbreath, and Jim Miller. The children are pictured with their Christian flyers and bibles. (Courtesy of Laura Duffield Biegger.)

This photograph shows a Sunday morning service at the Methodist Episcopal church. As the preacher finishes up his sermon, the choir prepares for its next selection. Fresh flowers and lighted candles adorn the chancel area. The shades are drawn in the sanctuary to keep the morning sun from distracting worshippers. (Courtesy of Laura Duffield Biegger.)

The Methodist Episcopal and the Christian churches were the only denominations represented in Altoona for many years. The Methodist Episcopal church was organized on May 9, 1869. The services were held in the railroad depot with 109 conversions in seven weeks. Later, the congregation met in the Woodrow School House, one mile from town. The church building was completed in 1870, and the church members worshipped there until 1909, when the building was moved 15 feet west and a 20-foot-by-30-foot addition was constructed on the west side. The tower was moved from the front of the original part and replaced where the old and new wings met. The parsonage was built in 1881 and 1882 and served until 1953, when a new parsonage was added. It was home to 35 ministers and their families. Shown here is the church with a wooden walkway and the parsonage.

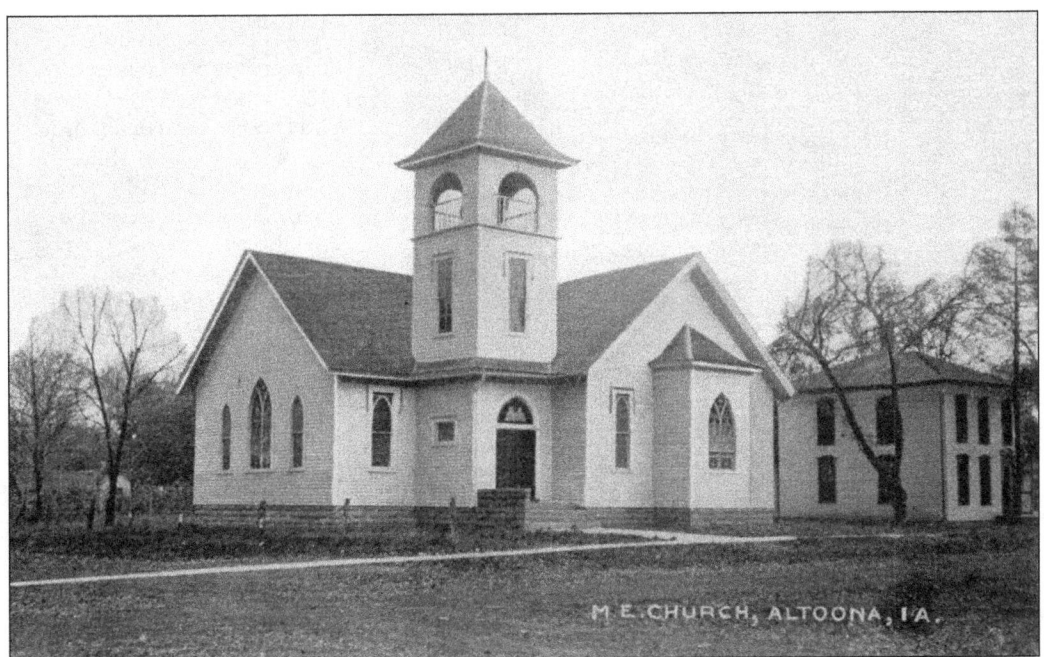

The early ministers of the Methodist Episcopal church were Jacob M. Holmes (served in 1869), John F. Guyle (1871), Walmore G. Boynton (1872), Ichabod T. Miller (1873), James W. Adair (1875), Miles A. Wright (1876), Horace W. Delshler (1878), Francis M. Slusser (1879), William E. Howe (1880), Elmer W. McDade (1881), and Francis Plumb (1883).

In 1922, a brick basement was constructed underneath the Methodist Episcopal church. This provided room for a fellowship hall, Sunday school rooms, and a kitchen for church suppers. Construction for a new church was finished in 1965 at 602 Fifth Avenue Southwest. The new church is a redbrick building on a 10-acre site with tall century-old tree. (Courtesy of Laura Duffield Biegger.)

It was early in his ministerial career that Rev. Elmer McDade served the Altoona Methodist Episcopal Church. He was the pastor there in 1881 and 1882. When he left Altoona, he served in neighboring Prairie City and then several Iowa towns—Clarinda, Perry, Red Oak, and Atlantic—before ministering in Des Moines from 1915 through 1940.

Christ the King Lutheran Church held its first Sunday service on October 6, 1974, under the direction of Rev. Robert Schoolcraft. The service was held at the Altoona Methodist Episcopal Church. The church building was erected in 1976 at 600 First Avenue North and is still home to the parishioners today.

Howard Jones, son of Adam "Bill" and Clara Jones, is shown here with his two 4-H fattened Black Angus steers, preparing them for show. Halter training and grooming were part of the regimen. He was under the guidance of Eugene "Shake" Ford. Shown in the background of this 1940s photograph is the barn on the family farm, located north of Ivy.

Shake Ford (right) stands with two boys in the Altoona 4-H group in front of their display in the Altoona Hy-Vee, the current location of Pat Barton Dance Studio. Their group was called the Hustling-Herdsmen. Ford, nicknamed "Shake" by the townspeople for his love of Shakespeare, was the 4-H group's leader for more than 30 years.

The Altoona Kitchen Band was formed to help celebrate the Altoona centennial. This performance took place in January 1968. All band members were required to have a kazoo and a homemade instrument but were allowed to wear whatever outfit they chose. The band performed nationwide, including the Iowa State Fair; Hawaii, Illinois, Kansas, and Minnesota; on a Caribbean cruise; and at political functions. They even entertained a group of Soviets walking through Iowa in 1988 and were featured on television. The last performance of the Altoona Kitchen Band was at the Altoona Elementary School on October 24, 1999, the place of its first performance.

The Altoona Kitchen Band is one of the most famous and well-known organizations in Altoona's history. It is seen here in the Altoona centennial parade, which took place on Saturday, July 27, 1968. The parade was held at 9:00 a.m., and the band played at 3:00 p.m. during the four-day celebration, lasting from Thursday, July 25, to Saturday, July 28. The band was featured in *Life* magazine, gaining national fame.

The Adventure-Life Reformed Church had its first service under founding pastor Gary H. Vande Kamp on September 10, 1978, in rental facilities at 319 Eighth Street Southwest. In August 1979, the congregation rented another building for worship. On October 28, 1984, church members held their services in their present brick church building at 1700 Eighth Street Southwest.

This is the ground-breaking service for the Altoona Methodist Episcopal Church on Sunday, June 7, 1965. From left to right are district superintendent Dr. Merril Summerbell, representing the Conference Cabinet; Dean Stump, chairman of the Building Committee; J.W. Porter, one of the oldest members of the congregation; and Pastor Richard Bentzinger.

The Altoona Masonic Lodge got its charter in June 1881. Before that time, men living in the Altoona area joined Masonic lodges in Des Moines or Mitchellville. In this 1921 class, L.O. Shaffer, Malcolm L. White, Eddie S. Cree and Leroy V. Porter are from the Altoona area. Shaffer, Cree, and Porter later transferred to the King David Masonic Lodge in Altoona.

Four
Events and Entertainment

Fourth of July celebrations in Altoona have been major events in the past, bringing together the entire city for food, games, and entertainment. This image shows Betty, Lewis, Ann and Barbara Heller waving flags during the 1925 Fourth of July celebrations in Altoona. Live music, baseball games, fireworks, and other various activities were common during the celebrations at the time.

Fourth of July used to be a major celebration in Altoona, as it was in 1906. This program was printed by the *Altoona Herald* and includes advertisements for Porter Brothers Hardware & Implements, Haines Park Hotel, Altman & Son Grocers, Citizens Bank, Frank Crawford Meals and Rooms, and Phil Yant's Groceries and Dry Goods. The planning committee that year consisted of John Kelley as president, J.W. Porter as secretary, N.B. Shaffer as treasurer, Henry Gifford as chief marshal, and T.E. Haines and Lewis Shaffer as the reception committee. The activities included a pie-eating contest at 1:20 p.m. where the first-place prize was 75¢. Other activities of the day included a ladies' nail-driving contest, a ladies' ball-throwing contest, and a ladies' 25-yard race. A game of tug of war took place, and the winner went home with a box of cigars.

The Great Train Wreck of 1877 was one of the deadliest in Iowa history. In August 1877, major rainstorms flooded central Iowa, including Little Four Mile Creek. On the night of August 29, the creek was a raging stream 50 feet wide at the point where it crossed the railroad. The pencil sketch below was made shortly after the train wreck. The Barnum Circus poster car was the first into the creek, killing seven Barnum crew members. A total of 17 people lost their lives, and more than 40 were injured. P.T. Barnum himself came to Des Moines on September 10 of that year to help raise money for Cottage Hospital, the local hospital in Des Moines. The hospital was the main location victims were transported to after the accident.

This photograph was taken during the Acme Day celebration on June 22, 1911. It was organized by Porter Hardware to display the Acme machinery it sold. In May, the store had received a carload of Acme binders, mowers, rakes, and hay tools. The Acme Company began in 1860, but Porter Hardware was a recent seller of its products. Porter had tried Acme out in 1910 and found it to be reliable. The Ancient Order of United Workmen (AOUW) Military Band furnished music all day, and the Helping Hand Society furnished nearly 150 dinners for Acme customers and their families. Twenty-eight Acme binders and 10 mowing machines were delivered that day to area farmers. Following dinner, teams were hitched to the binders and mowers, and automobiles decorated with flags and banners lined up to participate in a procession led by the AOUW Military Band. After traveling from First Street to Third Street and back to First Street, the binders and machinery were lined up to have a picture taken. Afterward, lemonade and cigars were passed out, and the crowd dispersed. The event brought over 500 people to Altoona.

This tornado struck Altoona on May 28, 1899, at 3:00 p.m. This is one of the earliest photographs of a tornado, taken by J.C. Plummer of Altoona. The light effect of the long, rope-like cloud is due to the sun shining against it. It was reported that the tornado touched the top of Mr. Prunty's grove and moved on to John Rick's farm with increased force. His barn was torn to pieces, and several horses were injured. The funnel had damaged many homes along the way to the Skunk River when this picture was taken. The cloud then lifted once again and moved on to Mingo, where it damaged several buildings and killed much livestock. Chimneys, machine sheds, and barns were destroyed by the tornado. No lives were lost in the Altoona area, but one woman was killed in Keswick, Iowa. Five others in the area were injured. A great deal of damage was done to the growing crops.

Willowbrook Place is an Indian village on the western edge of Altoona. It was started by Jim Poweshiek, the great-grandson of Chief Poweshiek of the Fox tribe, also known as Mesquakies of Tama, Iowa. He built the village out of white elm bark, with certain pieces from linn and basswood trees. Willow was used for poles. Jim lived there during the summer and conducted tours for the many visitors. In the photograph above, Jim strings pumpkin on a pole in the village. Jonas Poweshiek, son of Jim, was born on the Sac and Fox tribal lands at Tama, Iowa. He was a member of the Grizzly Bear clan of the tribe. He and his wife, Ruth, raised their family in Altoona.

Jonas Poweshiek had a love for education. The village was a place of learning for Iowa schoolchildren, and powwows were held there. In addition to showing Indian life in the village, Jonas was employed at the Iowa State Historical Museum and created most of the Indian displays there. He lectured to hundreds of thousands of Iowa schoolchildren at the state historical building in Des Moines over a 31-year period. His talks on Indian lore and history drew many visiting students each year. The children of Jonas and his wife, Ruth—Gloria, Nadine, Richard, and Edgar—were an integral part of the village activities. Gloria and Nadine are seen above, and below, the children watch their mother do beadwork.

Altoona was home to the first municipal airport in the state of Iowa. The Des Moines Aviation Park was created on December 7, 1926, on the current location of Adventureland Amusement Park. The airport was also known as the Altoona airfield or Hanna airfield, named after the owner of the land, James R. Hanna. The City of Des Moines leased the 160 acres of land from Hanna for $2,700 a year. On August 27, 1927, Charles Lindbergh dedicated the airport. Besides Lindbergh, Amelia Earhart and Art Gobel also made appearances at the airport. The 1928 air shows included wing walking and parachute jumps. These shows would draw people from all corners of Iowa. Attendance at the annual air show totaled 50,000 people. In 1933, when the Des Moines airport on Fleur Drive opened, the Altoona airport was abandoned.

Boys from Altoona would ride their bikes across town to the airfield to watch the different air shows and the everyday activities taking place with the different planes flying into and out of Altoona. For those who did not wish to make the journey over to the airfield, they could view the activity from the roof of the Old Grimes Canning Factory.

This scene at the Altoona airfield was taken on August 27, 1927, as Charles Lindbergh dedicated the airfield. There were no runways, and planes could land wherever they wished. Lindbergh also went to the Iowa State Fair during his stop in Altoona. Altoona was one of several Iowa cities Lindbergh visited on a nationwide tour promoting aeronautics.

Shown in the picture are Laura Duffield and her father, Gordon, holding up a homemade cardboard sign as Adlai Stevenson's black motorcade drives by their home along Highway 6 next to Mud Creek. Stevenson was on the way to Des Moines on September 18, 1952, for a speech downtown. He had come from Newton, another presidential campaign stop along Highway 6. The Colonial Bread sign shown in the picture was a promotional item supplied by the Des Moines baking company. Stevenson served as the governor of Illinois before pursuing a presidential bid and later served as US ambassador to the United Nations. He was known as a very eloquent speaker and a liberal candidate. Some of the topics Stevenson spoke about in Des Moines that evening were corruption in government, taxes, and inflation. He ran for president in 1952 and 1956 under the Democratic Party, never successfully winning the bid. (Courtesy of Laura Duffield Biegger.)

The centennial celebration took months of planning and hundreds of volunteers and lasted four days. Featured events on Youth Day (Thursday) included a parade, the crowning of the queen, foot races, a greased pig race, and a treasure hunt. On Farm Day (Friday), a spinning demonstration, a tractor-pulling contest, and a threshing demonstration took place. Old Settlers Day (Saturday) brought a small tractor pull, a fiddlers' contest, and skydivers. Sunday finished out the celebration with a muzzle loader demonstration, a variety show, a magician, and fireworks.

This photograph shows one the Za-Ga-Zig Shiners entry in the centennial parade in 1968. The Shriners are a prominent civic-minded organization with a meeting facility in Altoona. The parade featured 170 entries that included 1,062 people, 142 horses, 54 ponies, and 5 mules. The parade route was 1.5 miles long.

The centennial parade tools down Second Street with a 1929 Altoona hose truck that was still in service. The buildings in the background are present-day home to the Class Act Productions Theatre and the Altoona Area Historical Society. The crowd includes a wide variety of people from farmers to Shriners.

Dressed for the Altoona centennial parade in July 1968 are, from left to right, Elias Heller, his sister-in-law Florence, and brother George Heller. The Hellers were from a prominent family in Altoona and were involved in local community and business interests. They are seen here in the staging area for the parade. Pictured in the background is the Altoona Elementary School.

During Altoona's four-day centennial celebration in 1968, demonstrations such as weaving and spinning, muzzle loading, oat shucking, and threshing were offered. Fashion shows featured models in old wedding dresses, women's bathing suits that covered more skin than was shown, and old football uniforms. Fun activities included greased pole climbs and a greased pig chase.

In April 1926, Barbara Jane Heller had a birthday party with her first-grade class and their teacher. They enjoyed outdoor games, and lunch was served by Anna, Barbara's older sister. There was a 7:00 p.m. family dinner with their teacher, Doris Snyder, as a guest. Pictured from left to right are Anna Heller, Betty Heller, three unidentified girls (two seated, one standing), Barbara Heller, Doris Snyder, Marjorie Owens, and Warren Owens.

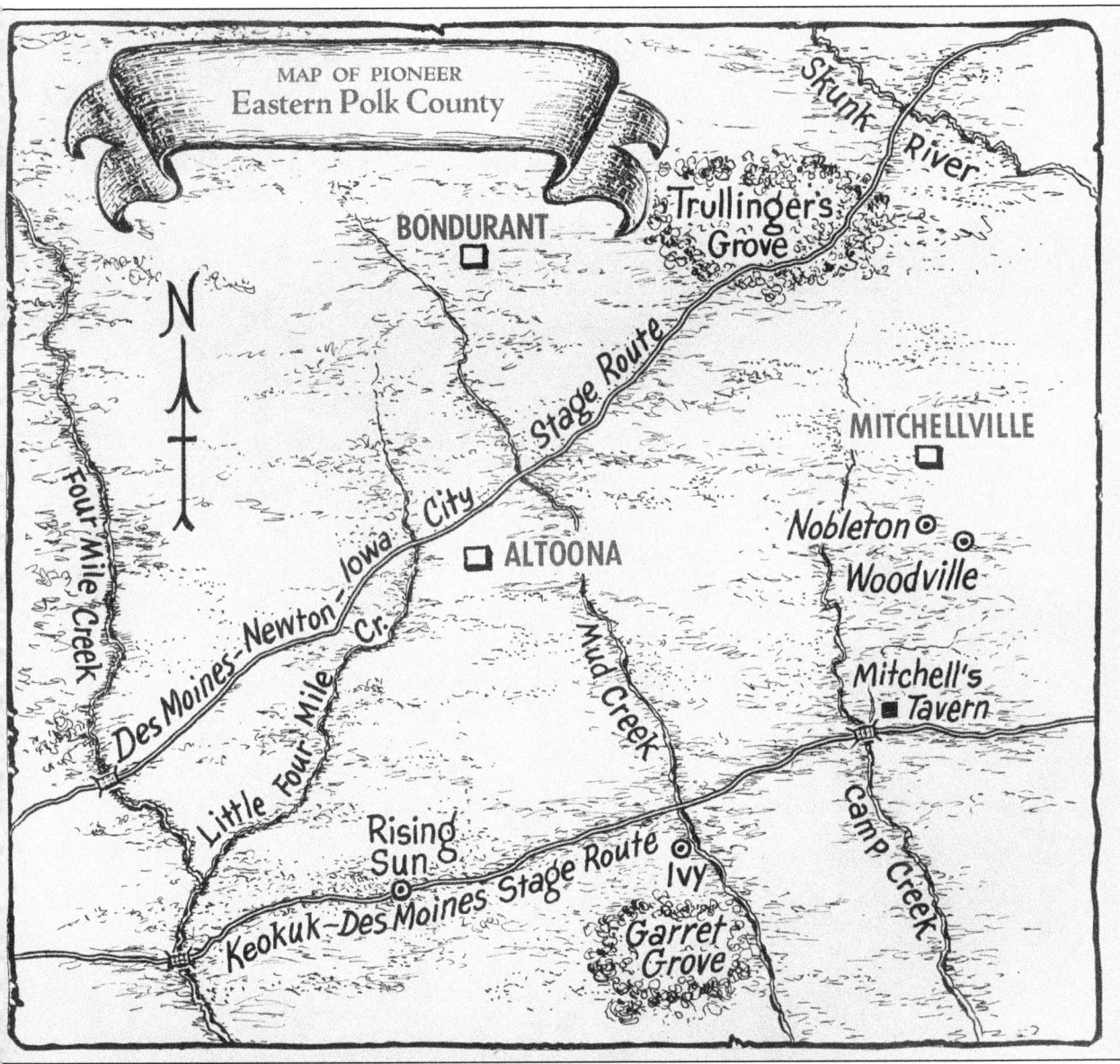

Frink and Walker operated the first stagecoaches in Iowa. In 1854, the Western Stage Company took over the stage lines. Stagecoaches delivered mail and transported people. There were not any stamps in the early days of mail delivery. To save on weight, people wrote on both sides of the paper, and it was folded so a blank spot ended up on the top of the letter; the delivery address was written in that spot. The cost to send a letter was based on the weight of the letter and the destination, and the letter was stamped to show the fee paid. Postage stamps were not introduced until 1847, and they were not required until 1855. In November 1857, the state capital was moved from Iowa City to Des Moines. The stagecoach transporting the safe with the treasury gold became stuck in a slough along Little Four Mile Creek, just east of Tenth Avenue Northwest, in Altoona. The safe contained all the state's reserves. It was stuck for several days before being pulled out by 10 yoke of oxen.

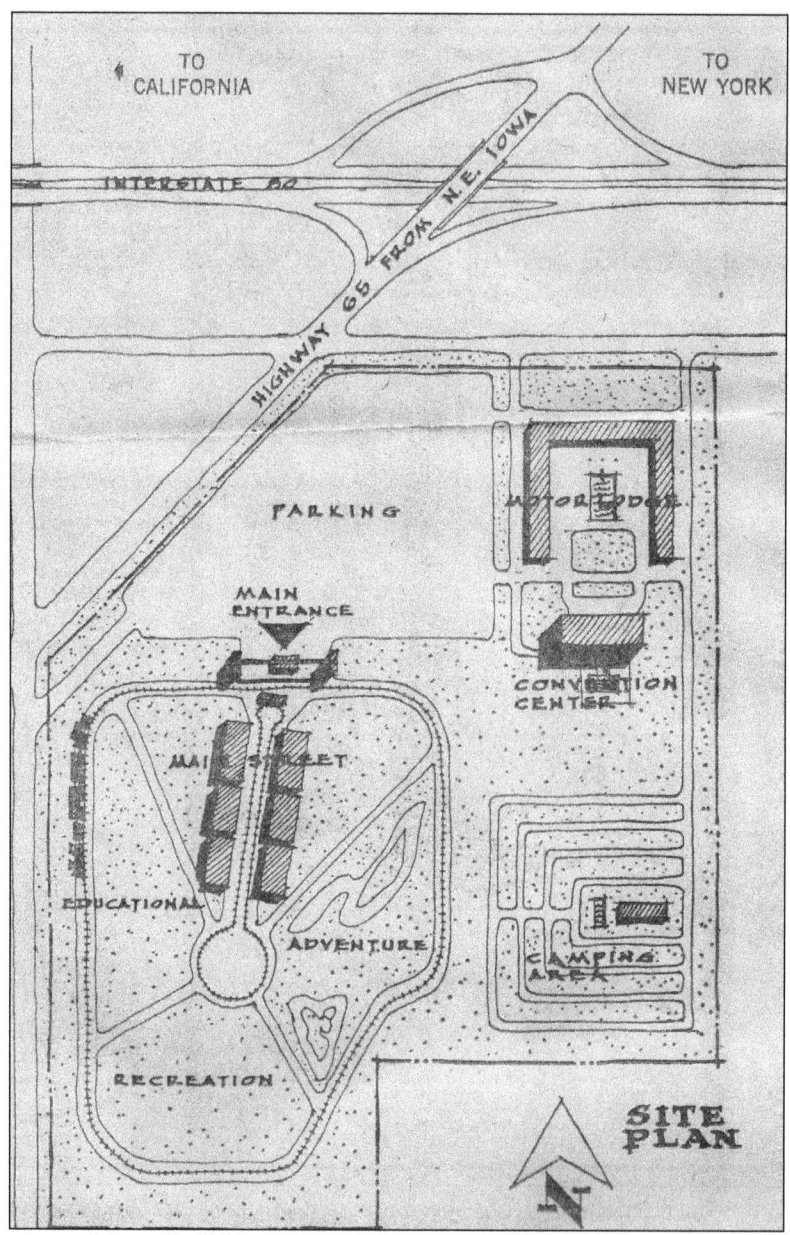

This 1971 plan for Adventureland Amusement Park shows the many different sections of the proposed park. Several designs were changed before the park opened to the public in 1974. In the fall of 1971, Adventure Lands of America, Inc., president and chief executive officer Jack Krantz appointed H.E. "Jerry" Phelps as project manager and Dale Schlenk as administrative manager. The two were based out of St. Louis at the time and were involved in the same capacities in the construction of Six Flags over Mid-America in St. Louis. The park was to be divided into sections including Main Street, Adventure, Recreation, and Educational and include rides, attractions, displays, and exhibits of general appeal. It was proposed that a section of the park be made available to Iowa manufacturers to display the growth of Iowa and its part in the economy of the nation. The Main Street section still contains specialty shops with unique architecture, such as gift shops, fashion boutiques, restaurants, and a theater for stage and film presentations.

Barney the Bandmaster, one of Adventureland's many characters in the mid- to late 1970s, entertains a group of visitors to Adventureland. The Main Street section of the park was designed to be like an Iowa town square around the early 1900s. Adventureland president and chief executive officer Jack Krantz, along with local artists, traveled around to 120 Iowa towns to take photographs of old buildings to reproduce at the Adventureland site. (Courtesy of Alex Payne.)

Leo the Lion hangs off of a trolley at Adventureland, overlooking Main Street. The trollies were built in the barn at Adventureland in 1973 by Gordon Woligrocki. The structures on Main Street represent buildings around Iowa. The schoolhouse resembles one that was razed in 1954 in Nevenville. The firehouse was based off of one in Pella, and a hotel in Burlington was the design for a corner gift shop. (Courtesy of Alex Payne.)

When Adventureland opened in 1974, trollies encircled the entire park. Trolley stops included the train station at the front of the park; a second stop between the current locations of the Inverter and Der Flinger; and a third stop where the current entrance to the Tornado is. (Courtesy of Alex Payne.)

Main Street USA at Adventureland has stayed similar to when the park opened on August 19, 1974. The grand opening of the park was delayed after a tornado earlier that summer damaged Main Street, blowing out the windows of the buildings. The section shown in this photograph in the mid-1970s is the same area that was completely lost to a fire on February 20, 2010. (Courtesy of Alex Payne.)

The Silly Silo was one of the last original Chance Rotor rides left before Adventureland removed it at the end of the 2013 summer season to make way for the new ride called the Storm Chaser. The Silly Silo was a staple since the park opened in 1974. The ride used centrifugal force to "plaster" riders to the sides of the cylinder-like room before the floor would drop out below riders. The ride had an operating speed of 35 revolutions per minute and could hold a total of 30 adults. The Silly Silo was in the Farm section of the park. The park was originally designed to also be an educational park. Next to the Silly Silo is the Wee Critters petting zoo and the John Deere museum in the barn behind the petting zoo. Rotors were introduced in the late 1940s by German engineer Ernst Hoffmeister. Rotors were exhibited throughout Europe during the 1950s and 1960s. They reached their popularity in the 1960s and early 1970s. (Courtesy of Alex Payne.)

Poppy's Place at Adventureland has since been turned into the Iowa Café. Poppy's Place was a unique place for finding food right off of Main Street at Adventureland. Poppy's was named after the interior decorator and architectural designer for the park, Don Popplestone. Evidence of Poppy's, like light fixtures and decorations, is still in the Iowa Café. (Courtesy of Alex Payne.)

This section of the park was the back boundary until the expansion of Riverview Island (now Dragon Island) in 1979. In this image is Sheriff Sam's Saloon, named after the former mayor of Altoona and Polk County sheriff Sam Wise. The sky ride was a gift from the 1974 World's Fair held in Spokane, Washington, for the park's first full season in 1975. (Courtesy of Alex Payne.)

The Tornado roller coaster at Adventureland was considered one of the top 10 wooden roller coasters in the nation after it debuted July 4, 1978. The coaster was built by the Frontier Construction Company but devised by world-renowned coaster designer William Cobb. The Tornado is an out-and-back-style coaster that curves around Adventureland's small lake. (Courtesy of Alex Payne.)

The Adventureland campground was the first to be completed of the three-part family resort complex. The campground, completed in July 1972, is shown here with an Olympic-sized swimming pool and a campground store. The campground still brings many people to the area annually to camp and enjoy a weekend at the amusement park. While the park was being built, workers and their families lived in the campground. (Courtesy of Alex Payne.)

The original *Iowa Great Lakes Queen* riverboat pictured is docked in the River City section at Adventureland Park. Jack Krantz bought the historical boat, which was on Lake Okoboji in northern Iowa, and had it towed 196 miles down to Altoona. The *Queen* was on Lake Okoboji for 89 years before it moved to Altoona in May 1973. The Adventureland lake was lined with an underwater track for the *Queen* to ride on, taking riders on a 20-minute tour around the lake. Townsend Industries helped with the construction of the track and underwater installation. The *Queen* sat in its docking place for a few years before it disappeared. Tales of what happened to the *Queen* range from sinking it with dynamite to burning it down. The River City area of the park is currently part of a food court area. The docking station for the *Queen* has since been turned into a barbecue and lemonade stand. (Courtesy of Alex Payne.)

Five

PEOPLE AND HOMES

Anthony Yant, born in Pennsylvania, married and started his family in Ohio. He was one of the early settlers who came to the Altoona area in 1854 and bought 320 acres of land north of Second Avenue Southeast. He held the offices of justice of the peace and township supervisor. One of the first names for Altoona was Yant's Station.

Thomas Haines was born in Ohio in 1831, one of nine children. He came to Iowa in 1863 with his brother and 4,000 sheep. In 1868, he sold his farm and moved to Altoona doing business as a grain dealer. He married Loretta Berridge in 1869. Soon after, he built the elevator, providing the town with a much-needed service. During his lifetime, he also owned a tile and brick plant as well as land. Four acres were donated for a city park bearing his name. Haines was active in civic affairs, including the Altoona Christian Church, and was a Clay township trustee as well as serving as a state legislator in 1882 and 1883. Haines believed in women's rights and Prohibition. He was instrumental in forming the King David Lodge. Haines and his wife did not have any children of their own but raised Minnie Van Wey and adopted niece and nephew Nellie and Guy Berridge. Haines built the Haines Park Hotel in 1902. The couple spent the remainder of their lives in Altoona; Loretta died in 1895, and Thomas followed in 1908.

George Heller was born in Illinois in 1879 to Benjamin and Harriet Heller. George received his education from an Illinois college and earned a diploma from pharmacy school, which he completed in 1902. He began working in farming with his father for two years in Polk County and then spent 10 years of traveling for three companies. He transitioned from farming to public service, and from 1915 until 1933, he served as the deputy Polk County auditor. This move kicked off his career in accounting for several different public offices. He was associated with Altoona city government as councilman from 1920 until 1936. He held the mayor's office continually from 1936 until 1953 and served in public office for one third of a century. He and his wife, Florence, did not have any children.

This 1900 picture is of the Ford family. Pictured from left to right are (first row) Hiram Ford, Rose Ford, Walter "Sticks" Ford, and Mary Daniels Ford; (second row) Dale "D.B." Bert, Charles "Chick" Ford, and Eugene "Shake" Ford. Hiram, a Civil War veteran, was a bricklayer and had a house moving business, which his son Shake continued. Shake lived his adult life in Altoona. He was born during the year of America's centennial and died the year of its bicentennial. He had two nicknames: "Shake," because he loved Shakespeare in high school and quoted the writer throughout his life, and "Popeye," which he was called by the children he spent his life mentoring as he kept a pipe in his mouth. He taught Sunday school and led 4-H groups for many years. He never married and lived in a log cabin south of Altoona.

Growing up during the 1940s in a small town like Altoona was very different than today. During the summer, children left home in the morning and came back for supper. Their friends' moms would feed them lunch. There was an air of innocence. Kids did not have to worry about getting kidnapped—only about getting caught. The boys played marbles and jacks, made forts, and spied on girls. There were baseball games and rock fights. On very special occasions, children shared a bottle of pop and a candy bar. These boys' fathers all worked for the Rock Island Railroad. Above, from left to right, are Bob Scharf, Dennis Slutts, Martin "Junior" Johnson, and Conley Slutts (sitting in front) in the Slutts family's backyard. In the c. 1945 image seen below are, from left to right, Junior Johnson and Dennis Slutts as well as Dennis's dog. (Both, courtesy of Mary Jane Johnson Buck.)

The Johnson family takes a break on a bench. From left to right are Mary Jane, father Martin, mother Lillian, and Junior. The family came to Altoona when Martin's job on the Rock Island Railroad moved him to Altoona as track supervisor. The family lived in Altoona for 10 years before moving to Des Moines and then out of state. Their home still stands at 206 Fifth Street Southwest. (Courtesy of Mary Jane Johnson Buck.)

Farmer Carl Eshelman was born in neighboring Bondurant, Iowa, in 1887. Along with farming, he served as a rural mail carrier out of Altoona for 35 years. When he started the mail route, wagons were horse drawn, and there was no pavement and very little gravel—just black dirt. His route was 61 miles long.

Rose Lucas lived to the ripe old age of 99. She was born in Knoxville, Iowa, in 1879. She married William D. Vertz in 1898, and they had five children: Winifred, Thelma, Lillian, Paul, and Leona. William and Rose ran the Vertz Grocery for 34 years. The store was in two different locations on the same street over the years. One family story from the grocery business involves a particular customer whose credit was overextended. When the customer came in to make another purchase, William denied him additional credit. The customer became irate and said he was going home to get a gun, but William said he would just end it now. Before the customer walked out the door, William took two fake sticks of dynamite and threw them into the potbelly stove. The customer ran away and never came back.

Four generations of the Wheeler, Shaffer, and Heller families are shown in this 1913 photograph. In the picture are baby Lewis Heller, his mother Edna Shaffer Heller (directly behind Lewis), Edna's mother Carrie Wheeler Shaffer (right), and matriarch Melvina Hemstreet Wheeler (left), who was 71 at the time this picture was taken. These ladies were prominent in the Altoona community.

James O. Mason and his wife, Mary, came to Iowa in 1856, living in a cabin in Fort Des Moines. In 1870, the family moved to a farm near Altoona. Hiram Mason, one of Mason's sons, was in the hardware and general merchandise business. Son Ortis Preston Mason was a hardware and grocery merchant. Son James was the editor of the *Altoona Herald* from 1900 until his death in 1945.

James B. Porter was a farmer. He lived west of Altoona where four generations of Porters have lived. He and his wife, Sarah Ann Kinney, had seven children. They were members of the Altoona Church of Christ. He was a member of the King David Masonic Lodge in Altoona.

Jeremiah D. Williams is pictured with his wife, Martha M. Hawkins. They married in Polk County upon his return from the Civil War. Jeremiah came to Iowa from Indiana with his parents in 1850 and moved his family to Kidder County, North Dakota, during the 1880s. He returned to Altoona before 1900 and owned several businesses, including a meat market with his son-in-law Albert Immel.

This senior photograph is of Gene Harding, who graduated from Altoona High School in 1948. Harding played on the high school football team and served in the Korean War. Harding came from a large family and lived at 202 Third Street Southeast, near the Christian church. He married Norma Daugherty, and they had three children. Harding was an executive with Principal Financial in Des Moines. (Courtesy of Mary Jane Johnson Buck.)

Betty Blake's 1948 graduation picture is shown here. Her parents owned the Red Arrow Café on the corner of Eighth Street Southwest and Third Avenue Southwest in Altoona. The café featured hot meals as well as a full-service filling station. Sold in the 1940s, the Red Arrow Café eventually became a Maid-Rite restaurant. (Courtesy of Mary Jane Johnson Buck.)

John Kelley came to Iowa from Ohio with his parents in 1882 at the age of 10. He taught at a rural school and then became editor of the *Altoona Herald* from 1894 to 1900. He was deputy sheriff of Polk County for six years and served as a state representative in the Iowa Legislature for two years and then as superintendent of the state archives in the State Historical Building in Des Moines for two years.

Martin J. Blesz, born in Hungary in 1903, came to the United States in 1907 through Ellis Island. He worked as a farmhand and attended Des Moines University. Having purchased the newspaper from Mate Mason, widow of James Cletus Mason, who was a longtime publisher of the paper, Blesz became owner, editor, and publisher of the *Altoona Herald–Mitchellville Index* for 22 years, from 1945 to 1967.

Born in 1862, Lewis Olney "L.O." Shaffer, a druggist and banker in Altoona, arrived from Indiana with his parents and settled on a farm near Altoona in 1875. Lewis was only 13 years old when his father died. In 1878, at the age of 16, Shaffer became associated with Dr. William Booth in the drug business in Altoona. Shaffer had just graduated from a college of pharmacy. In 1885, he bought out his partner and took over the business himself at the age of 23. In 1888, he built and occupied a brick storeroom. He added to his property year by year until he had one of the finest drugstores in the county. He owned four business properties as of 1901 on Second Street Southwest. In 1901, when he bought the Altoona Exchange Bank from Robert A. Crawford, he also bought the eight-room residence of Crawford on First Street which was next door to his then-present residence. Shaffer died in 1950.

Altoona residents Eileen Shannon and George Benjamin, who both lived near Largey School, attended classes together and were high school sweethearts. They married after high school and had three children. George went into the service and served during World War II. He was also a meat cutter for Charlie Graves. This picture was taken in front of Eileen's parents' home. (Courtesy of Mary Jane Johnson Buck.)

Mary T. Porter was born in 1855 in Jasper County, Iowa, and died at her home in Altoona in 1937. She taught in the rural schools around Altoona before marrying Hiram S. Mason in 1875. The couple lived on a farm before moving to town in 1896. Mary taught Sunday school for over 40 years at the Church of Christ and was member of the Order of the Eastern Star. She and her husband had two sons.

Summertime in Altoona meant homemade ice cream in the Duffield home. This photograph shows Laura Duffield enjoying the fruits of her father Gordon's labor. Laura was not the only one who enjoyed the chocolate ice cream; the family cat was caught licking ice cream off the lid. This picture was taken in the 1950s. (Courtesy of Laura Duffield Biegger.)

Laura Duffield and her cousin Craig Redshaw often swam and caught minnows in Mud Creek on hot summer days when he came for visits from Des Moines. The picture was taken about 1952 at Laura Duffield's home, located just east of Altoona on Highway 6. Mud Creek ran through the family property. (Courtesy of Laura Duffield Biegger.)

Junior Johnson was born on January 6, 1936. He is shown here sitting on the concrete steps where his mother, Lillian, would bring graham crackers outside of the kitchen door, on the back of the house facing the J.W. Porter home. Junior would enjoy his snack out in the warm summer sun after a nap. (Courtesy of Mary Jane Johnson Buck.)

Mary Jane Johnson and Norma Champion met and quickly became friends in 1937 when the Johnson family moved to Altoona. The two remained friends throughout school and continue to be friends to this day; their friendship has lasted over 75 years. The two were Camp Fire Girls together. Here, they are seen in the backyard of the Champion home. The Champions had a cow named Daisy in the city limits before laws prohibited it. (Courtesy of Mary Jane Johnson Buck.)

Nicholas Hemstreet was born in New York in 1815. He moved his wife, Ellen, also born in New York, and children west to Wisconsin, where he worked as a farmer and a blacksmith. In 1868, the family again moved, this time to Iowa, settling in Altoona. Hemstreet built one of the storerooms and opened a general store that sold dry goods, boots, and shoes among other things. He continued in the business about three years and then retired to live a more quiet life. He owned farmland of about 300 acres, all improved land, besides his house and other property in the city. He was the justice of the peace elected in Altoona. Ellen is 81 years old in the picture.

William Sanford Carpenter was born in Iowa in 1871. He married his wife, Lenora, on June 25, 1894. Both Carpenter and his wife were physicians. His medical office was at his home in Altoona, where he also performed embalming services. He was the Iowa state coroner for over 40 years. Carpenter moved to St. Louis, Missouri, prior to 1940, where he owned and operated a school of mortuary sciences.

The Altoona ladies wearing white dresses are, from left to right, Melvina Wheeler, Harriet Heller, Edna Heller and Martha Casebeer. They are attending an Epworth League Assembly camp meeting at nearby Colfax. In 1909, it was held August 5 through August 15, with opening session speaker Carrie Nation, a very outspoken proponent of Prohibition. The crowd numbered over 1,000. The Epworth League Assembly is a Methodist association.

Roy Davis Sr. had running service stations in his blood. His father owned a station in Mitchellville. Davis Sr. had two gas stations in Altoona. His son Roy Davis Jr. later owned and operated his father's White Way Sinclair Station. The station switched to selling Phillips 66 gas.

This is three-year-old Lewis Heller in 1916. Note the buggy in the background. Lewis is the grandson of L.O. Shaffer and the oldest of five children of Elias and Edna Heller. Lewis grew up in Altoona before getting married and moving to Los Angeles with his wife, Pearl. He died in 1970. His career included being a machinist.

Melvina Hemstreet Wheeler, born in 1842, is shown cutting up meat that was preserved in the wooden barrels. Meat was typically salted and placed in barrels in a cave or cellar, where it was kept cool before the time of refrigeration. Melvina's death in 1932 marked the passing of the last charter member of the Methodist Episcopal church in Altoona.

Benjamin F. Heller was born in Ohio in 1842 and died in 1927. His wife, Harriet Alford, was born in Illinois in 1845 and died in 1945. Both deaths occurred in Altoona, and they were married 64 years. The family and their eight children moved to Altoona in 1902. In 1910, Heller owned a farm and was a traveling salesman for a creamery and silo business. Benjamin served as justice of the peace for Altoona from 1915 through 1920.

The George Heller home in this photograph is located at 205 Third Street Southeast. The five-room home was built in 1900. The bay window pictured in this 1938 photograph has since been removed, and the porch has been enclosed. This southeast-area home was valued at $2,500 in 1940.

This house at 207 Sixth Street Southwest was built in 1903 and still stands today. Jesse and Nellie Porter, owners of Porter Hardware, one of the major businesses in Altoona from 1902 to 1982, lived here. The store was on the main street, Second Avenue Southeast. They had two children. They had one child, named James "Ralph" Porter. After the death of his father, Ralph continued operating the hardware store until it was closed.

Pictured is the L.O. Shaffer house, which still stands at 204 Second Street Southeast. Lewis married Carrie Wheeler in 1882. They had three children. One daughter, Edna, married Elias Heller, while their son, Norman, married Frances Wilson. Norman was a state bank examiner and became president of National Bank in Chicago. Their other daughter, Anna, married Everett Stivers, a high school aeronautics teacher in the Chicago area.

This house was located at 102 Third Street Southeast on property next to the G&G Grocery, which was on First Avenue South. Both were owned in the early 1900s by Clark Pearson. This small house is a typical modest dwelling of Altoona. It was torn down in 2004 for a commercial building. (Courtesy of Karen Hanley.)

The William Barber house was moved to 206 Third Street Southeast about 1938. Barber, an Iowa native, was a telegrapher for the Rock Island Railroad. In addition to their natural son, Barber and his wife adopted a daughter and took in a neighbor's son as a foster child. In 1930, the value of the house was $2,100. The house is still standing.

This house at 204 Second Street Southeast was built in 1924 for the L.O. Shaffer family. Shaffer, a druggist and banker in Altoona, graduated from the College of Pharmacy at Des Moines University in 1878. He immediately went into the drug business, in which he continued for 30 years. He started the Citizens Bank in 1900, and in 1901, he bought the Altoona Exchange Bank.

This rural home was the first farm of Elias W. and Edna Shaffer Heller. Pictured to the left is the summer kitchen. The photograph includes, from left to right, Benjamin F. Heller (father of Elias), Clarence Laney, and Elias W. Heller. This photograph was taken around 1913.

This is a two-and-a-half-story foursquare home with four large, boxy rooms on each floor, dormers, and a large front porch with wide steps. The rural Altoona home was owned by the Hammers. There are chickens in the yard, a barn in the background, and a farm wagon on the right side of the picture. Flags fly on the porch.

This rural brick Altoona house is located at 8357 Northeast Forty-sixth Avenue. The one-bedroom, one-bathroom home was built in 1928 and owned by Gordon and Vera Duffield. They raised their family there and had livestock. In addition to their home, they had 30 acres of land. This picture was taken during the early 1950s. (Courtesy of Laura Duffield Biegger.)

This picture was taken at the rural Altoona home of David and Marcella Wheeler DeVotie. In 1870, still a single man, David documented a cattle drive from Fairfield, Iowa, to Colorado he embarked upon with two other men. Pictured around 1884 from left to right are Cornelia, her mother Tamar DeVotie, Duane DeVotie, Worthy DeVotie, Lillian DeVotie, and Roy DeVotie, the children of Marcella and David DeVotie, who are pictured at right.

In this photograph is the house of Thomas and Loretta Berridge Haines. This 19th-century Victorian home still stands today at 202 Second Street Southeast near the Olde Town section of Altoona. The house began as one Thomas built for his bride, Loretta, in 1869. They lived in the house, and as Haines prospered, he remodeled, adding on to the west side of it. There were many parties held in the home, and when it was renovated, it became Altoona's first modern home. After Loretta's death in 1895, Thomas married Samantha Achey. He died in 1908, and in 1919, Samantha sold the house to Dr. William Carpenter. The original part of the house was sold and moved to a new lot several years later, at which time Dr. Carpenter constructed additional living space and an office in the remaining part of the house.

This is a typical modest house in the early 1920s and 1930s in a small town. It has a barn out back with a cupola. Perhaps the builder of this house still farmed beyond the city limits but kept his machinery in town when he and his wife moved into Altoona. This was a rental house in the 1940s and 1950s. (Courtesy of Karen Hanley.)

This rural Altoona barn is a classic example of a Midwest design used by many farmers with abundant livestock. It was typical for farmers to be pictured with their animals to show their prosperity. Notice the large, well-maintained barn. A cupola was not usually added to a barn, as the expense was not practical. Lightning rods were placed on barns to prevent fire from lighting strikes during rainstorms.

Six
Public Services

Thomas E. Haines was a prosperous Altoona citizen. In the 1880s, he donated about four acres to the town for a park. He had in mind to use it himself to exercise his horses but also wanted the town to have an area for recreation. As park commissioner, Haines would announce times when the townspeople could graze their cattle in the park.

The Altoona Service Roll, seen here in the fall of 1943, had three additional columns of names added after 1943. Names included on this board were those of veterans of the Civil War, World War I, and World War II. The service roll was located on the site of the current Class Act Productions (CAP) Community Theatre and former home of the American Legion hall built in 1948.

John H. Kelley was a well-known Altoona resident. For seven years, he was publisher of the *Altoona Herald*. He was also a deputy sheriff for six years and served two years as a state representative. Kelley returned to the sheriff's office as chief deputy in 1913 and remained there until 1931. He was justice of the peace from 1937 to 1958 and a Mason for 50 years. He lived until the age of 89.

This 1968 view of First Avenue looking north reveals a glimpse of history. On the left are the Farmers Cooperative, a sign for Altoona Ready-Mix Concrete Co., and the Conoco gas station with a gas price sign reading 31¢ and 35¢. The right side shows an empty grain bin and the Iowa Department of Transportation building.

The Altoona Post Office was built in 1959 and dedicated on September 26 by Congressman Neal Smith. The one-story, brick-and-block building sits at the corner of First Avenue and Third Street Southwest, formally the Ingalls property. The post office served the community until moving to the current location on the corner of Third Avenue Southeast and Eighth Street Southeast in July 1986.

The fire station and town hall were completed in February 1928 and located on Second Street Southeast in Olde Town. The west side of the building consisted of the mayor's office and a 22-foot-by-24-foot council room. The east end was occupied by one city fire truck and one township fire truck. After the fire station moved to its current location, it was bricked in, as shown in this photograph.

In 1962, the new fire station was built, moving it out of the city hall building, which is now the Altoona Area Chamber of Commerce. This new fire station had a capacity of four trucks and a meeting room. This photograph was taken after the 1966 addition of the town maintenance facility.

The construction of the city hall was approved in 1976. A budget of $200,000 was allotted. The next year, the City of Altoona approved an additional $25,000 to complete the building. There were offices for the mayor, police, and the city clerk. City council meeting rooms are used by the community. The city hall is located at 407 Eighth Street Southeast.

This 1968 photograph shows the Iowa Department of Transportation building located at 405 First Avenue North; it is still currently in use. The building houses the maintenance equipment used by State of Iowa road crew employees to clear snow, sand streets, and maintain gravel roads in the area.

In this picture of volunteer firemen taken in 1951, are 21 of the 31 men who trained and donated their time in the case of an emergency. During the year preceding this picture, the largest number of fire calls were on farms, where such incidences occurred as machinery spreading sparks to dry crops and machinery catching on fire. Barn fires were common, as were grass fires, due to a stray cigarette or spark from the wood stove. The water supply caused a problem in that it was inadequate. In March 1951, the firefighters asked Altoona area residents to help fund a tank truck to go out to fires with the fire trucks. A firemen's ball was held as a fundraiser in 1951. An ad for the ball said, "Your contribution is an investment for personal fire protection. Prevention is the best cure."

These fire trucks, the one above from the 1930s and the one below from the 1940s, were Altoona's fire equipment in 1951. These pictures were part of an ad about Altoona's need for a tank truck to go with the engines to rural areas. The tank truck was of more importance than replacing either of these engines. "Help Us Help You" was the volunteers' motto. They were having a ball to raise money in this instance. Other fundraisers were oyster and chili suppers. The fundraisers were to buy equipment, repair equipment, and study firefighting methods. Since the firemen were not paid, the ad says a pat on the back was appreciated.

Zilla Hick willed her 900-square-foot home to the city to become the Altoona Library at 700 First Avenue South in 1969. When the second library building was constructed in 1984, Hick's home was sold and moved to 300 Sixth Street Southwest. The second library was erected on the same lot as the first library building had been on before it was moved. It was dedicated on July 1, 1984, and had a capacity of 31,000 books. This new building became the police station when the current library was built in 1998 at 700 Eighth Street Southwest. It was constructed at a cost of $3.2 million and is nearly four times the size as the previous one. Amongst the library's supporters are the Jaycees, the Lambda Tau chapter of the Beta Sigma Phi sorority, the ACTION Committee, the American Legion, the Lions Club, the Women's Connection, and individual contributors.

These pictures are from the open house for the 10-year anniversary of the library in 1979, which coincided with national library week and a short program honoring Faith Kurtzweil. The event was held on April 11, and light refreshments and snacks were served. The history of the library was shared, as was pleasant conversation among the community members who attended. For 37 years of her 45-year teaching career, Kurtzweil taught in a Waterloo High School and was one of the certified student counselors in the state. She grew up in Altoona and spent her life serving the community as well volunteering as librarian for many years.

Altoona had several wells in the business district for public use during its early years. The water supply was sufficient during years of adequate rainfall but fell short during dry spells. This rotary drill opened a well during the winter of 1967–1968. The cost of the project was $100,000. The well was put into operation in April 1968 with Altoona mayor Sam Wise flipping the switch on the pump.

The ribbon cutting for a senior center at 119 Second Street Southeast is seen in this picture. The old city hall on Second Street Southeast was given to the seniors. The Lions Club helped sponsor the center, while rent and utilities were paid for by the city. In 1980, the city provided a van to be used by the senior citizens and shared with the Altoona Recreation Department.

Sam Wise, born in 1918, was very active in politics and city government. He served as mayor for a total of 18 years and as Polk County sheriff. The Sam Wise Youth Complex was named after him for all of his efforts on expanding Altoona Parks. He was instrumental in paving the city streets as well as building a sewer system with expansion in mind. He died in 1991.

Tim Burget is Altoona's longest-serving mayor, serving in public office from 1978 to 2011. During his 24 years as mayor and 8 years on the city council, he attended nearly 1,000 council meetings and chaired over 800. In 2003, Burget founded the Altoona Area Historical Society. In 2006, the city purchased the former Porter Hardware building to house the Altoona Area Historical Museum. (Courtesy of Tim Burget.)

This log cabin was situated in Haines Park from 1921 to 1967. Painted on the front of the cabin on the chinking (small sticks and rocks) between the logs is "Welcome to Altoona." Log cabins were built by stacking horizontal logs. The gaps between the logs were typically filled in with chinking and mud. The cabin sat on the southeast side of the park.

This winter scene in Haines Park features Altoona park board members, from left to right, George Loupee, Norman Turnquist, and Robert Thompson as they consider a site plan and changes as well as cleanup to be made in the park. Two local Cub Scout leaders assisted in removing dead trees and brush.

A lagoon was created in Haines Park by the dredging of a swamp on the park grounds. Formed within the area was an island with a bridge that connected it with the rest of the park. Haines himself had a boat he kept on the lake. The park was a popular place for swimming and fishing, and local churches performed baptisms at the lagoon. A well and windmill helped supply water to the park. Schoolchildren and the townspeople contributed their time to the development of the park by planting trees. The lagoon is long gone, as it was drained many years ago, but the depressions in the park are still very evident.

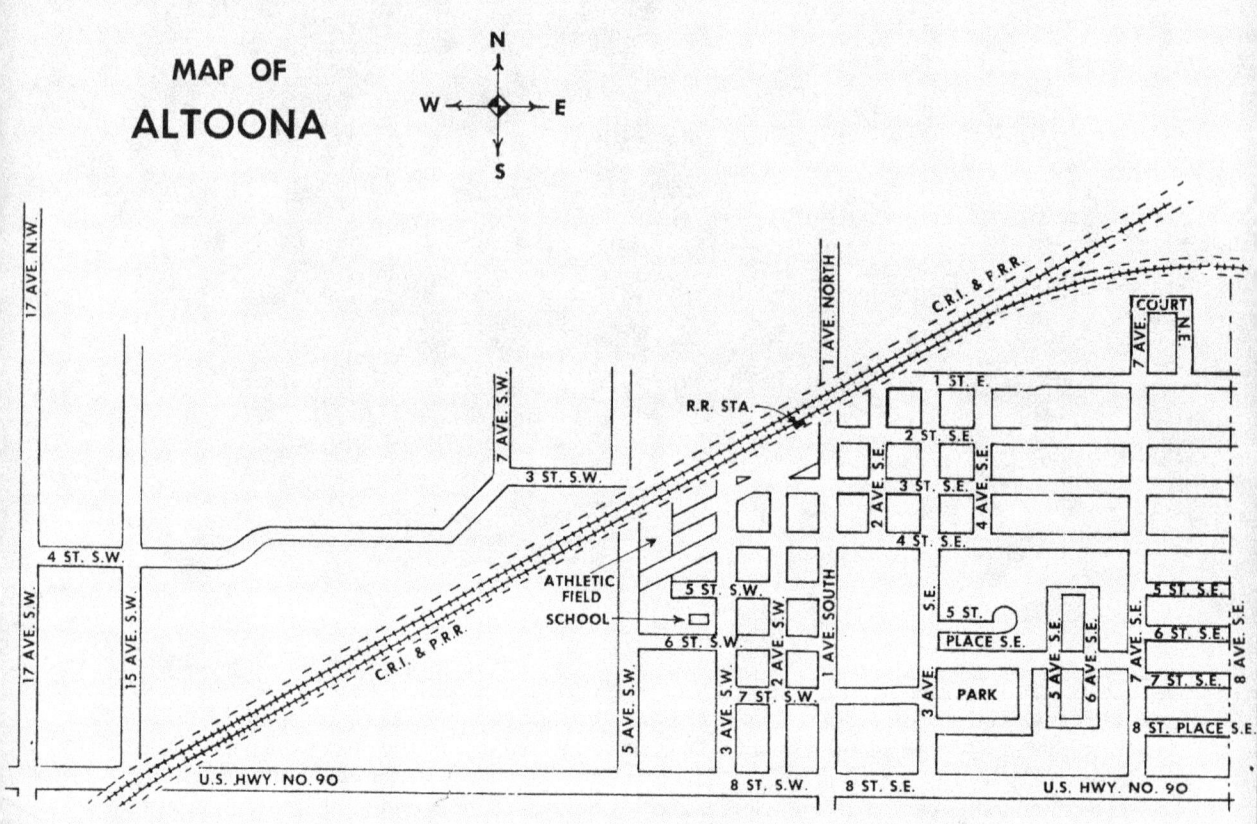

The City of Altoona was revolutionary in developing paved streets. This plan was lead by Mayor Sam Wise and brought a literal roadway for businesses and families to move to Altoona. Wise's forward thinking made Altoona one of the forefront cities in the Des Moines area for roads, sewer, water, and fiber optics. Many of the street names have been changed over the years. This map shows the street system. Shown is the south section of the city streets. First Avenue is the divider between east and west. On this map, the Altoona School and school athletic field are visible. Haines Park is pictured just off Third Avenue, and the railroad station is also indicated on the map. The current-day avenues were once all named with actual names rather than numbers. Some of Altoona's avenues once boasted names such as Grant Avenue, Main Street, Davis Street, Yant Street, and Beaver Street.

About the Altoona Area Historical Society

The Altoona Area Historical Society operates the Altoona Area Historical Museum at 104 Second Street Southeast in Altoona. On May 5, 2003, the Altoona City Council recognized the Altoona Area Historical Society as the city's official organization to collect, secure, and preserve the artifacts and records of the city of Altoona and surrounding areas. To find out more information on the historical society and/or to schedule tours of the museum, contact them at www.AltoonaHistory.org. All of the royalties made from this book will be donated to the historical society for continued preservation efforts at the museum.

Visit us at
arcadiapublishing.com

Printed in the USA
CPSIA information can be obtained
at www.ICGtesting.com
LVHW081249051024
792932LV00004B/323